Sweden – Inside Out

A snapshot briefing
on the country and its people

Anita Shenoi

Kakao förlag

Published by
Kakao förlag
Stadt Hamburgsgatan 9B
211 38 Malmö
Sweden
www.kakao.se

Text: Anita Shenoi
Editor: Sharon Zink
Printing: Göteborgstryckeriet, 2009
Paper: Munken Polar, 150 g
ISBN 978-91-85861-16-3

Contents

Sweden – inside out

I was fifteen when I had my first real taste of a Swedish summer: a picture-book delight of lazy, sunny days spent splashing about in sparkling clear water, surrounded by unspoiled countryside. My penfriend from Linköping had invited me to stay, and we'd gone off for a few days to her grandmother's cottage by lake Vänern. The classic, red cabin had absolutely no mod cons to speak of – no electricity, shower or flushing toilet. And it was wonderful. We brushed our teeth with lake water, barbecued sausages and stale bread over an open fire, and rowed a little wooden boat over to a tiny, uninhabited island where we could sunbathe in splendid isolation.

For me as a young British teenager, going back to nature was a completely new experience. For many Swedes, however, this is *de rigueur* – a simple but given holiday pursuit, scheduled for any time between the June solstice and the September equinox. But is there more to Sweden than pine forests, pristine lakes and tall blonds, attractive as they all might be?

As you peruse the following pages, the answer to that question might just amaze and amuse you. And it might just turn a misconception or two on its head. Whatever you already think about Sweden, prepare to take a look at it from the inside out…

A brief note on the format of this book
As you read, you will notice key words or concepts highlighted in **blue**. These are either described in the main text and/or further explained in the key word section at the end of the chapter.

Sweden – not Switzerland

Scrolling down to S in the list of countries on the CIA World Factbook website, I find Sweden sandwiched between Swaziland and Switzerland. While it's unlikely anyone would confuse Sweden with a small, landlocked country in Africa, many do confuse it with a small, landlocked country in Europe. And, I'm ashamed to say, the most confused seem to be the Brits and the Yanks. So let's begin by getting our facts straight, courtesy of the Central Intelligence Agency of the United States.

First we learn that Sweden is over ten times the size of Switzerland, and is thus pleasantly put on par with the Sunshine State. Things get sunnier still when the factbook reveals that Swedes have three-thousand two-hundred and eighteen kilometers of coastline at their disposal, whereas the Swiss have to be content with a smattering of big lakes – geographical advantage Sweden.

Delving further into 'transnational issues', however, really separates the watchmakers from the ironmongers. Although both countries have enjoyed a long (and crooked) history of neutrality, only one merits CIA classification as 'a major international financial center vulnerable to the layering and integration stages of money laundering'. You've guessed it – the watchmakers win in the corruption stakes.

SWITZERLAND
Location: Central Europe, east of France, north of Italy
Geographic coordinates: 47 00 N, 8 00 E
Total area: 41,290 sq km
Comparative area: slightly less than twice the size of New Jersey

SWEDEN
Location: Northern Europe, bordering the Baltic Sea, Gulf of Bothnia, Kattegat, and Skagerrak, between Finland and Norway
Geographic coordinates: 62 00 N, 15 00 E
Total area: 449,964 sq km
Comparative area: slightly larger than California

In fact, Transparency International's 2008 Corruption Perceptions Index ranks Sweden joint first with Denmark and New Zealand as the least corrupt countries in the world. Apparently, the Swedes are rather good at making the bribery of foreign civil servants difficult. Not surprising really, as the nation has a penchant for policing and can sniff out the foibles of its government officials like bloodhounds sniffing out fugitives.

Nevertheless, that same nose for monkey business is aided by a mind defaulting to consensus and everyone has the Swedes to thank for inventing the *ombudsman*. No wonder then, at least in public life, they have a reputation for being polished bureacrats whose steely diplomacy is admired worldwide.

Did you know *that the Swedish loan word ombudsman is derived from the old Norse umbuðsmann, meaning representative? The term was first used in the modern sense when the Swedish Parliamentary Ombudsman was instituted in 1809, safeguarding the rights of citizens by establishing a supervisory agency independent of the government. However, official ombudsmen in a variety of capacities existed much earlier in Scandinavian history.*

But what about in private? Do all Swedes beg to agree, not to differ? Are descriptors such as 'honest', 'conflict-shy', 'reserved', and 'unemotional' fair to the nation? How did the descendants of battle-axe-bearing warriors become home-loving pacifists? A glimpse into the history of the Swedes might help us begin to answer these questions.

Did you know that Carl Bildt was an early advocate of the Internet as a means of communicating? On 4th February 1994 he wrote an email to then U.S president Bill Clinton – an email which has been publically acknowledged to be the first ever between two heads of government.

Home Swede home: the rolling countryside of Österlen, Skåne is where many Swedish celebrities choose to live in the summer. Dag Hammarskjöld (UN Secretary-General 1953-61) bought a home here.

DIPLOMATIC DYNAMITE

Folke Bernadotte was a Swedish diplomat noted for his negotiation of the release of approximately 15,000 prisoners from German concentration camps during World War II. After the war, Bernadotte accepted an urgent appointment by the United Nations Security Council to mediate in the Arab-Israeli conflict of 1947-1948. Sadly, he was shot down by a terrorist gang during his mission.

*Having served as prime minister of Sweden from 1991-1994, **Carl Bildt** went on to work internationally as a mediator in the Balkan conflict, first as the European Union's Special Envoy to the Former Yugoslavia and later as the United Nations Secretary-General's Special Envoy for the Balkans.*

From cut-throat cads to squeaky-clean Swedes

With very little documentation to go on, apart from the boastful heroicism of the sagas, it's easy to understand why modern culture is fascinated by the idea of the Vikings as the bone-crunching, blood-drinking world terrorists of the Dark Ages. However, many popular notions about these Nordic adventurers have been perpetuated by the romanticism of the nineteenth century; a time when some historians let unreliable sources and their unfettered imaginations get the better of them.

Since the word *vik* means inlet or fjord in all Nordic languages, the etymology of the word *viking* suggests it refers to a 'man of the fjords'. However, from the Old Norse sagas we learn that '*fara í víking*' means 'to go on an expedition', and *víkingr* referred to a seaman or warrior taking part in such a mission. Some were pirates, others were traders, but most were probably an adventurous mixture of the two. Holger Arbman, a well-known Swedish archeologist of the past century, gives us one of the simplest definitions: 'The viking was a combination of robber and merchant in nordic ships along foreign coasts'. 'Foreign coasts' constituted any lands outside Scandinavia accessible by ship, as far west as the Northern American continent and as far east as the Caspian Sea. While 'Norwegian' and 'Danish' vikings

WRITTEN IN RUNES...

The Scandinavian fuþark is a runic alphabet, the origins of which are unclear. Apart from being etched into stone to commemorate the dead, mark territory or tell of important events, runes were used to inscribe people's names on personal items such as jewelry, combs or weapons. Runes were even used for idle graffiti wherever the literate loitered, whether they were robbing ancient tombs or carving rude messages into the walls of old stave churches.

Tryggr carved these runes
Ingigerth is the most beautiful
of all women

Of the 6,000 runic inscriptions known in the world today, approximately half date back to the Viking Age. In Sweden alone there are more than 2,500 runestones, one of the most famous being the *Rök* runestone in Östergötland. The province of Uppland, which includes the northern part of Stockholm, has the highest concentration of runestones in the country.

largely expanded westward and southward, 'Swedish' vikings expanded eastward, and the explosive movement in all three directions occured almost simultaneously during the period 800 to 1100 A.D.

The Vikings' heyday came to a close with the absorption of Christianity, and Scandinavians started looking inwards instead of charting new territory. For Sweden, conversion to the new religion was slow and it was not until the latter part of the eleventh century that it had the country in its grasp. The eleventh century is also the period in which a great number of runestones were raised, the association perhaps having been more than coincidental. Runic memorials had long been purely pagan, but this time Swedes were using the stones to assert the Christian character of their deceased relatives.

Did you know *Swedish nobility formally became hereditary for the first time in 1561? No hereditary titles or honours have been granted since 1902, and the Swedish monarch lost the right to ennoble in 1975.*

Fact or fiction?

The Vikings waged war in horned helmets.
Fiction There is very little evidence to suggest vikings wore horned helmets. If they did wear them, they were ceremonial at best. Instead, findings link such headgear to the Celts, bronze helmets having been uncovered in England and France.

The Vikings had a reputation for being a particularly clean people.
Fact In England, vikings had a reputation for excessive cleanliness, due to their custom of bathing once a week. The local Anglo-Saxons didn't really believe in washing their bodies much and were bemused by the Norsemen's Saturday ritual. The grooming customs of the Varangians (vikings who went east) are also reported on by 10th Century travel writers of the Islamic world.

The vikings were noted for their wild binge drinking and liked to use human skulls as cups.
Fact and fiction The vikings loved their liquor, which is not surprising considering the harsh conditions they were exposed to. However, they used horns for drinking, not skulls, the latter misconception probably arising from a mistranslation of Old Norse. The word skál (skål in modern Swedish) simply refers to a bowl.

This shift away from exploration and conquest towards looking inwards meant much squabbling between the Scandinavian kings until the Kalmar Union between the Nordic countries at the end of the fourteenth century brought some stability. Over the next hundred years, however, internal turmoil bubbled up again, and the campaign for Sweden to be a nation in its own right culminated in the election of Gustav Vasa as king in 1523. From then on, it was full-sail ahead into the Age of Greatness. The Swedes had been in possession of Finland since the fourteenth century and by the sixteenth, had moved on to make attempts at controlling Estonia, Poland, and other strategic spots around the Baltic. Nevertheless, persistent clashes with Denmark eventually wore Sweden down economically, as did tussles with Russia, and it was forced to hand over Finland in 1808. A few years later, the Swedes actually sided with the Russians against Napoleon and quickly went on to take possession of Norway, which had been under Danish rule.

Did you know a Swedish law passed in 1620 made it illegal to emigrate from Sweden? Restrictions were not completely lifted until 1860.

Luther rules with the law of Jante

Lutheranism came to have a significant role in shaping the attitudes of the Swedish state and its people. Back in the 1520s Gustav Vasa was quickly attracted by the secular rather than the theological advantages of the ideology, but getting his Catholic citizens to accept The Reformation proved tricky. It was not until 1593 that the Lutheran creed was officially agreed upon for the nation.

Once it took root, however, the religion was with Sweden to stay; an undercurrent in the psyche of a nation which later turned out to be one of the most godless of the twentieth century. Lutheranism, with its denouncement of financial wealth and the 'sins' this entailed, suited the egalitarian Swedes very well. They had never succumbed to serfdom, and despite continental influences, the privileges of the nobility were few. Eliticism was out, honesty and hard work were in. Above all, being **lagom** (moderate) was what life was about.

These values later became interwoven with the ideals of social democracy in the nineteenth and early twentieth centuries. While the positive effects of this development were to reduce much of the poverty and social injustice of the time, the negative effects of treating everyone the same led to some individuals feeling an increasing sense of personal curtailment.

The pressure to conform and play down personal strengths is a sentiment the Danish-Norwegian writer Aksel Sandemose would describe and define as *The Law of Jante* in his 1933 novel *A Fugitive Crosses his Tracks*. The law consists of 'Ten Commandments', all of which can be summed up in the statement: *Don't think you're anyone special or that you're better than us*. Although this attitude had been an integral part of Scandinavian life long before Sandemose coined the concept, twentieth-century Swedes, Norwegians and Danes now had a term they could use to talk about it. Some deny its existence in a modern, more international Scandinavia; others still wince when they are reminded of its subtle presence in places of work or education.

Kiruna: breaking new ground
above and below bedrock

Since its creation as the 'iron ore' capital of Sweden in 1900, Kiruna has been vital to the industrial growth of the nation. During World War II there was a certain conflict of trade interests as the Allies and the Germans struggled to regulate exports from the region. The city's now on the move, not in anticipation of some fiendish foreign takeover, but because the ground is literally crumbling beneath the community's feet. Expansion of the mine means the centre of Kiruna has to be moved northwest to the edge of lake Luossajärvi, in a carefully phased manoeuvre to be conducted over the next few decades.

Kiruna is moving upwards too – perhaps not in terms of high-rise buildings but certainly in its estimation as a centre for international space research, benefiting as it does from the activities of the ESTRACK tracking station and the Swedish Space Corporation. In 2009, the European Space Agency observation mission, CryoSat-2, will be launched from Kiruna to survey floating sea ice thickness and the surface of ice sheets. The three-year project aims to fill in crictical gaps in scientists' understanding of how global warming is impacting on polar ice cover. Kiruna's high latitude position makes it ideal for satellite monitoring – and for viewing the fantastic light display of **norrsken** (aurora borealis).

In the words of the nineteenth-century bishop and poet, Esias Tegnér, 'peace, vaccination and potatoes' followed. A population explosion and a series of disastrous harvests resulted in widespread poverty and hunger, precipitating the emigration of nearly a million Swedes to the USA in the fifty years or so leading up to the First World War. Having been slow to embrace industrialisation, Sweden remained very much an agricultural society, unable to cope with this new crisis. It also remained very Lutheran, and the lack of religious freedom was yet another incentive for emigration.

So, with Swedes seeking freedom in America, it was time for some radical reform. Emigrants returning to visit Sweden often contrasted the opportunities available to them abroad with the limitations of living in their native country, thus fermenting discontent at home. The threat of a great 'blood-letting' of the nation kick-started a reappraisal of Swedish society, laying the foundations for a generous social welfare system which would become world famous and for a period of rapid industrialisation that led to the country's achieving enviable economic growth in the latter half of the twentieth century.

Did you know that Sweden is the only iron-ore exporter in Europe, accounting for roughly 2% of the world iron-ore output?

KEY WORDS

Lagom This Swedish word means 'moderate', or 'just right', depending on the context. The term is also used to sum up the common Swedish tendency to avoid extremes in all aspects of life.

Modern Swedes are beginning to feel uncomfortable with this image of themselves, and many advertisements play on this sentiment. An example of this is the municipality of Botkyrka, outside Stockholm, which uses the tag line *Långt ifrån lagom* (hardly average).

Norrsken The 'northern lights', also known as aurora borealis, best seen in the polar region of the Northern Hemisphere during winter. The light display results from gas particle collision in the Earth's upper atmosphere.

*Borgholms slott, Öland. Eight-hundred years of Swedish
history has seeped into the walls of this magnificent castle.*

Personality matters

A convenient place, I think, to start a paint-by-numbers of stereotypes and assumptions, armed with the colouring box of leading questions and historical canvas of the last two chapters. Indeed, why not varnish the finished result with some serious research for good measure? But no. Lacking the anthropological astuteness of *Watching the English* (Kate Fox, 2004) or the native nous of *Swedish Mentality* (Åke Daun, 1996) the *Inside Out* approach is to take you down the path of shared observation, at this point stopping to inspect two of the most famous signposts of Swedishness.

THE IKEA UNIVERSE

When Ingvar Kamprad created his mail-order company back in 1943, no-one suspected the frugally-minded seventeen-year-old would go on to create a furniture empire spanning thirty-six countries and attain an estimated net worth of US$31 billion. *Nota bene*, the company never confirms estimates of its value, perhaps to confuse the Swedish tax office, which still can't work

---

Did you know *that you can get a whole house from IKEA? In association with local contractors, the BoKlok project is currently building residential developments in Scandinavia and the UK.*

Inside Out Tip
Don't try to spice things up by playing Devil's advocate at a social gathering. Pushing Swedes into giving their opinion when they're unsure of what everyone else thinks is like pushing them off a boat into shark-infested waters.

IKEA from top to bottom: Boklok house, Värmland.

out why the country's flagship of socialist-minded entrepreneurship operates as a Dutch charitable foundation or why its chairman is a resident of Switzerland (yes, Switzerland). However, IKEA does have its finger on the pulse of the people, producing everything for the home at prices everyone can afford. The trouble is, almost no-one can do flat-pack DIY as well as the Swedes...

FEELING AT HOME IN THE IKEA UNIVERSE MEANS YOU:

- Enjoy the in-store 'stamina test', which entails dodging hoards of screaming kids in the 'one way' system and queuing up for 'almost free' hot dogs once your blood sugar has dropped to a critical level.
- Regard regular trips to IKEA as a recreational activity and gain tremendous satisfaction from spending an entire weekend assembling a GRANKULLA futon for the spare room, only losing a few screws in the process.
- Are delighted when friends invite you over and serve dinner on identical plates to the ones you bought last month. They also have the same BILLY bookshelf in the living room, but you smugly notice they fitted the shelves back to front.

How many Billy bookshelves in Stockholm Public Library? Thankfully, none. The building and its interior was designed by architect Gunnar Asplund in the pre-IKEA era of the 1920's.

THE VOLVO WAY

Volvo Cars has been struggling with a slight inferiority complex of late. Unsatisfied with its deep-rooted brand image as the safe but boring family option, the company has been working hard to rev it up a little with new models such as the C30 and the XC60. It'll be a rocky road all the way though, what with the current economic climate and competitive-elbowing from the more style-conscious Saab.

Nevertheless, the Volvo way is all about commitment to the cause, as amply illustrated by the company's Swedish engineers in 2008. In a team bid to get Volvo Cars back on track, 75 engineers spent three months developing methods of cutting CO_2 emissions – on a completely voluntary, unpaid basis. They say the initiative, which devoured lunch hours and stole out-of-office leisure time, was their only way of surviving the current 'do or die' work climate at Volvo. Having modified a standard V50 in eleven respects, the team managed to produce the most fuel-efficient car in its class, achieving CO_2 emissions under 120g/km – the level proposed by the EU for new cars in the future. Whether those valiant Volvo engineers 'do or die' remains to be seen.

Did you know *that Volvo engineers aren't the only Swedes willing to work for free? In October 2008, a Nyteknik internet-magazine reader-poll revealed that 43% were prepared to work without pay if their company was in crisis and another 31% would follow suit if their bosses took the initiative.*

GOING AGAINST THE GRAIN – WOODWORK CLUB MORE POPULAR THAN THE PUB

Tired of meeting up for beers, a group of male friends in the Stockholm city district of Kungsholmen started up a woodwork club in an effort to find something to do that didn't involve alcohol. Describing the initiative as 'anti-trend' and a way of relaxing in an 'achievement-free zone', the group of young professionals also emphasise how they like to round off their carving sessions with a home-cooked meal. The club prefers to limit its size to a maximum of eight participants at each meeting, but outside interest in joining is so great, the organisers are hoping to inspire spin-offs around the city.

Making tracks the Volvo way means you:

- Wear a helmet and shin pads for your walk to work on an icy winter morning – never trust municipal road services to sand the pavements in time. And no, you're not driving because **a.** that half glass of wine you drank last night might still be in your system and **b.** you've delayed putting winter tyres on the V70.

- See it as a moral duty to impose your environmental fanaticism on everyone else, even if it compels you to hang around recycling stations in the hope of catching an old lady throw a frying pan in the wrong container, or to drive your partner insane by insisting (s)he rinse and put aside empty milk cartons instead of throwing them in the trash.

- Don't expect to be rewarded by anyone (including yourself) for being dilligent. After a week of slaving for the greater corporate good, Saturday is the day to finally take pity on yourself and your kids: they get to binge on a kilo of sweets, while you binge on Jägermeister and a six-pack.

Equipped with a little insight on IKEA-mindedness and Volvo vision, we should now feel ready to spend a little longer exploring the Swedish psyche – a whole year in fact – given that the mood of the nation is very much governed by the seasons…

Observer's corner

You've finally managed to get a first date with a Swedish hottie after months of investigative online 'chatting'. Does his/her preferred rendez-vous involve:

1 A boozy lunch at a flash restaurant followed by whatever the champagne-haze of the afternoon has to offer

2 Taking a water-colour class together – who knows how your creative talents will blend afterwards

3. A long walk *i naturen** followed by *fika** – perhaps you can bring a thermos of coffee, and they'll bring cinnamon buns?

see chapters 10 and 8 respectively

The glassy waters of Stockholm's archipelago.

When in Japan do as the Swedes

Dreaming of wooden houses, Dala-horses and Swedish crisp bread, but find yourself 7,500 kilometres east of your heart's desire? Then visit Tobetsu in northern Japan. In the residential enclave of 'Sweden Hills,' you'll find 350 wooden houses painted in traditional Falu red and inhabited by wealthy Japanese families who love the Swedish lifestyle.

Tobetsu has been twinned with Leksand in the Swedish province of Dalarna for over twenty years, during which time it has transformed itself from a grey Sapporo satellite town into a community pastiche of quintessential Swedishness. Stroll down Sweden Street and admire the pavements motifed with moose, viking helmets, and other Nordic symbols, or perhaps go and say 'Hej!' to the 2.5 metre tall Dala-horse stationed in its own pen in Leksand Park. For true Swedophiles, however, the Sweden Center Foundation in the heart of Sweden Hills is where it's at. The centre holds courses in the Swedish language, traditional baking and arts and crafts – to the delight of many a Tobetsu housewife.

While Japanese demand for Swedish building materials keeps four hundred Leksanders in work, there's very little chance of full economic reciprocity between the twin towns, unless tatami mats and paper walls suddenly become all the rage in a typical Dalecarlian home. In Leksand at least, a Japanese garden and a programme of Japanese cultural events will do...for now.

Did you know that the typical red paint used on wooden houses in Sweden is made from a residue containing over twenty different minerals from the now disused copper mines in Falun? Valued for its wood-preserving properties, Falu red has been used for centuries, but a limited supply of the raw materials means production can only continue for the next eighty years or so, at current levels of demand. The mining area of Stora Kopparberget (Great Copper Mountain) is a UNESCO World Heritage Site.

Spring into action

Suspended animation is not an unreasonable metaphor for life in Sweden during the first three months of the year. The only way to survive this frozen state of inactivity is to do what Swedes love best – plan ahead for the months that follow. Mental preparation starts with the popping of New Year champagne corks, and any lapses in optimism during February and March are remedied with the immediate intake of **semlor** – cardamom buns filled with whipped cream and almond paste. Originally only eaten on Shrove Tuesday, the 'Fat Day' favourites are now avidly consumed throughout Lent, without the faintest twinge of Catholic guilt.

Sweden's sugar high peaks at **påsk**, when children dress up as Easter witches and try to charm the neighbourhood into giving them as many sweets as possible, after which their parents ply

---

Did you know that the average semla contains 500 kilocalories? Swedes devour 40 million of these belly bloaters each year, but it's unlikely that any of them will stuff themselves to death as King Adolf Fredrik did on 12 February 1771, having eaten 14 servings of semlor and hot milk after a decadent lobster and champagne dinner.

them with more of the same, packaged in paper eggs. This custom and that of bringing birch twigs into the house and decorating them with coloured feathers date back to the nineteenth century. For the majority, such customs remain just that – customs without religious significance – although Easter is important to Swedes as a family occasion and a time to get excited about the first signs of spring.

There's nothing like a good bonfire to clear the stockpile of debris accumulated over the winter, and the blazes illuminating the night of **Valborgsmässoafton** (Walpurgis Eve) on 30th April are no exception. For most Swedish households, Valborg – as it is more commonly and conveniently known – marks the beginning of spring and the big spring clean that goes with it. Thawed out by a combination of fire and fire-water, many Swedes party into the small hours, freed from anxiety about getting up for work in the morning since 1st May is a public holiday.

Did you know that Walpurgis celebrations stem from Medieval traditions associated with the cult of Saint Walpurga? Bonfires were lit to keep witches and evil spirits away.

WEATHER WATCH

You can almost hear the trees groan with delight as promising green buds start to swell in April. Anticipation is in the air, the spring sun dazzling people into shedding scarves and unzipping heavy coats, only to regret it as soon as the cold air hits their winter-weary bodies.

Average maximum temperatures

	March	April	May
Stockholm	3	8	14
Gothenburg	4	9	16
Piteå	-1	5	11

Spring into shape or say goodbye to sporty Sweden?

The image of the fresh-faced Swede jogging before breakfast, power-walking through lunch, and playing ice-hockey after work is aging fast as a younger generation stays indoors with Xbox 360 and Nintendo Wii. This new wave of inactivity and the associated rise in child obesity has been blamed on Swedish schools, which now have less physical education on their curriculums than schools in most other European countries. Judging from the Swedish medal count at the 2008 Beijing Olympics (four silver, one bronze), the effects already seem to be setting in…

Did you know that the 1912 Stockholm Olympics gave Sweden its best ever medal count? On home ground, Swedes carried off 23 gold, 24 silver and 16 bronze medals.

SWEDES MIGHT NOT BE OLYMPIC HEROES AT THE MOMENT, BUT THEY ARE WORLD CHAMPIONS AT...

Tug-of-war Swedes won medals in all categories at the 2008 World Championships, of which four were gold, one silver and two bronze

Ventriloquism Nineteen-year-old Cecilia Andrén won the the Variety class at the 2008 World Championship of Performing Arts

Barber shop singing The Ringmasters quartet won the 2008 Bank of America Collegiate Barbershop Quartet Contest in Nashville, USA

Chainsaw handling Lasse Strandell has won gold at the World Logging Championships eleven times, and had top scores in all disciplines on several occasions

...and much more besides!

Seasonal Swedes

CARL XVI GUSTAF has been King of Sweden since 15th September 1973. Born on 30th April 1946, his birthday coincides with Valborg, and is therefore cause for double celebrations. As Crown Prince, Carl Gustaf met his future wife, Silvia Sommerlath, at the 1972 Munich Olympics, where she was an interpreter and host. The King and Queen have three children: Princess Victoria, Prince Carl Phillip and Princess Madeleine. Well, I never... Carl Gustaf is a bit of a Porsche fancier.

INGEMAR STENMARK (born in Joesjö, Lappland on 18th March 1956) is rightly regarded as the greatest slalom and giant slalom specialist of all time, having won these competitions an amazing eighty-six times at the Alpine World Cup, twice at the Olympics and three times at the Alpine World Championships. During his heyday in the late 1970s and early '80s, Ingemar became something of a Swedish folk hero – if he was in competition, people would stop whatever they were doing to gather round the TV or radio. Well, I never... As a child, Ingemar lived on Slalomvägen ('Slalom Road') in Tärnaby, now a popular ski resort. After many years abroad, he now resides for part of the year in Vaxholm on the Stockholm archipelago and is neighbours with ice-hockey legend, Börje Salming.

Ingemar Stenmark at the 1980 Lake Placid Olympics, where he won the gold in both slalom and giant slalom.

CARL LINNAEUS (23rd May 1707- 10th January 1778) is generally regarded as the 'Father of Taxonomy' for his work in establishing a universal standard for plant and animal classification. Although the Swedish naturalist did not actually invent binomial nomenclature, his survey of all then-known flora (about 7,700 species) and fauna (4,400 species) brought consistency and precision to the two-word naming system. Linnaeus' *Systema Naturae*, published in 1758, is still in use today. Well, I never... After Linneaus' son died leaving no heirs, his father's library, manuscripts and collections were sold off to Sir James Edward Smith who founded the Linnean Society of London. Sweden has been lamenting its cultural loss ever since.

Linnea borealis (Twinflower) is a fragrant woodland shrub, native to Sweden. Not only is it named after the great scientist, it is also the provincial flower of Småland, where he was born. The shrub starts flowering in May – just in time for Linnaeus' birthday.

Colour code your life the Swedish way!

It's a question of principle
In Sweden, the axiom, *'tänker blått, röstar rött, äter grönt och jobbar svart'* describes the sometimes paradoxical pick-and-mix of principles by which Swedes live. How do your colours match up?

Tänker blått Think **blue** (have conservative/middle class views)
Röstar rött Vote **red** (stick to socialist politics)
Äter grönt Eat **green** (make environmentally-sound consumer choices)
Jobbar svart Work **black** (work cash in-hand to avoid tax whenever possible)

Some days are red
Swedes like to refer to public holidays as **röda dagar** (red days), in keeping with the colour typically used to highlight them in calendars. With four *röda dagar* occurring between mid March and the end of May, employees look forward to years in which they fall on a Monday to Friday, thus making that all-important paid holiday go further. They also love to plan by week number, so don't be surprised if someone tells you, for example, that there are two red days in week 16!

Here comes the sun

If the Swedes have something to celebrate, then it has to be summer. Lighter days and lighter moods combine to make this the most carefree and fun time to experience the country.

The festivities kick off at the beginning of June with the end of the school year, which for nineteen-year-olds finishing **gymnasiet** is an excuse for public revelry of the highest order. Should you happen to be in one of the larger cities at the time, you may find traffic forced to a standstill by huge, open-top trucks, crammed with screaming teenagers wearing white caps. The carnivalesque atmosphere is contagious: if the kids aren't waving birch branches, they're waving beer cans, and you'll find yourself shouting and waving back or running for cover, depending on your frame of mind.

However, if the atmosphere seems a little damper on **nationaldagen**, it might be because Swedes haven't got used to celebrating their national day yet. Sixth June has only been an official public holiday since 2005, after a century of political debate. Gustav Vasa's election as King of Sweden in 1523 and constitutional reform in 1809 are given as reasons for celebrating, but the feeling that Sweden does not really have a story of liberation to tell (unlike its Norwegian neighbours) and ambivalence about the date's importance are two factors which have historically made a rainy day of it.

Many natives would, however, prefer to bypass the issue altogether and concentrate on preparations for **midsommar** – that Swedish celebration of light and lightheadedness, when floral wreathes and flowing dresses suddenly become acceptable attire for both sexes and people are encouraged to drink more aquavit than aqua.

Granted, celebrating the summer solstice is an ancient pagan tradition in Europe, but while most countries gradually succumbed to a Christianisation of the festival in the Middle Ages, Sweden was resistant. Although the church dubbed it St John's Eve, Midsummer's Eve belonged to the people, marking the end of the spring work season and a time of rest before hay-making. And Midsummer's Day continues to be the 'most closed day of the year', when working is almost considered a sin. For Swedes, at least, Midsummer is holier than Christmas!

MIDSUMMER ESSENTIALS

The main celebrations take place on Midsummer's Eve, occuring on the Friday between 19th- 25th June. Swedes have their own favourite venues for this – either the local village green or the privacy of their own summer houses. However, if you happen to be in Stockholm, head for Skansen, and prepare yourself for a spectacle. Because Midsummer is a spectacle. And because you might not be able to make head or tale of it, here's what you should know...

Inside Out Tip

This is **not** the time to sample nightlife in the capital. You will find the streets of Stockholm empty after mass exodus to the archipelago – surely an indication that the city isn't the glitzy metropolis it sometimes pretends to be. Major night spots such as Spy Bar, Café Opera and Debaser all shut at Midsummer, but the ever-stylish Berns has the good sense to stay cosmopolitan – and open.

Reeling ring dances

These are popular with small kids, or adults who've had enough to drink. An absolute favourite is *Små grodorna*, the melody of which can be traced back to a French Revolution military march. Ironically, the Swedish Embassy in Paris feels *Små grodorna* is so firmly entrenched in Swedish heritage, it has included knowledge of the song in its test of anyone applying for Swedish citizenship.

Know your nubbar

Apart from pickled herring, new potatoes and sour cream, Swedish schnapps is a must at Midsummer. Depending on where in Sweden you're celebrating, impress your hosts by bringing them a bottle of their local favourite, such as Gammal Norrlands Akvavit, Hallands Fläder or Östgöta Sädes Brännvin. That way, even though the numerous *nubbar* (shots) may leave you tongue-tied throughout the many drinking songs, you'll be the talk of the party.

Floral frolics

The light and ambiance of the summer solstice is truly special at this latitude. The twilight of a never-ending evening so intensifies the lush green of the summer foliage, you can't help but agree with the ancients about the magic of Midsummer. While they celebrated the supernatural with botanical rituals and fertility rites, modern revellers stick strictly to the symbolic gestures

Learn the lyrics and prove your worth!
Små grodorna, små grodorna är lustiga att se (x2)

The little frogs, the little frogs are funny to see.
Ej öron, ej öron, ej svansar hava de (x2)
No ears, no ears, no tails they have!
Kou ack ack ack, kou ack ack ack,
kou ack ack ack ack kaa* (x2)

*Swedish phonetic rendering of a frog croaking

WEATHER WATCH

Swedish summer weather is rather unpredictable. A scorching hot May might be followed by a drizzly June and in July, just as the water around the archipelago passes the toe test, you'll find a chilly breeze chasing you off the beach and back into the comfort of your wood cabin. Still, there's always time for a *brittsommar* in September or October – just ask Britta, whose name day marks the period in which Indian summers most frequently occur in Sweden.

Average maximum temperatures

	June	July	August
Stockholm	19	22	20
Gothenburg	19	21	20
Piteå	17	21	19

of making floral decorations and dancing around a leaf-clad maypole. Do not attempt to enact a more authentic pagan celebration – virgin sacrifices will not be appreciated. But as for any frisky behaviour, well, blame it on Midsummer madness...

WE'RE ALL GOING ON A SUMMER HOLIDAY

Once the delirium of Midsummer has died down, the country allows itself to lay back for a nationwide siesta, lasting over a month. The signs are everywhere: restaurants in the middle of town declare themselves to be **sommarstängt** (closed for the summer), buses adhere to a summer timetable and large businesses, previously buzzing with activity, snooze peacefully. Try arranging a meeting with your Nordic markets contact Britt-Inger at this time, and you'll find she's away from the office until September.

But in the modern world, this may seem like an exaggeration – it isn't. Since the Swedish summer is so short, natives have been genetically programmed to take time out and enjoy the one time of year when they can dispense with a woolly hat.

As you might expect, the laws of the country reflect this need. Back in 1938, *semesterlagen* was introduced to give employees the right to two weeks' paid holiday so that they would stay healthy and cope with the demands of working life. In 1940, even housewives got a break, the *husmoderssemester* holiday allowance enabling poorer women to get a few weeks of rest and respite.

Inside Out Tip

Don't worry, there's no need to get yourself into a networking frenzy to combat cottage envy. Just book one of the thousands of summer houses available for rent. A good place to start looking is the tourist office website for the region you intend to visit. For example, if you want to visit Västerbotten, go to www.visitumea.se.

Over the years, holiday entitlement was gradually increased, extending to a full five weeks in 1978. Thirty years on, there has been no change, even though there was a proposal to introduce six weeks' leave in 1989. Objections abounded – *lagom* is best!

Clearly then, summer is a precious commodity and the Swedes really know how to make the most of it. So what do they do with all this statutory freedom? According to a recent survey by the Swedish Environmental Protection Agency (Naturvårdsverket) walking is the most popular leisure activity. This may explain why 94% of those surveyed felt very strongly about the preservation of **allemansrätt** (public right to roam), which is also a major facilitator in the pursuit of other top ten activities, such as cycling, sunbathing, and swimming in lakes.

Interestingly, Swedes' second favourite activity is pottering around in the garden, and where better to do this than at the summer cottage? The idea of having a **sommarstuga** has appealed to Swedes since paid holiday came into existence and while not everyone owns one, they will know someone who does. If you're staying in Sweden for any length of time, don't be surprised when you receive an invitation to visit someone's third cousin's grandmother's house – if a Swede has the good fortune to own a *stuga*, it is only polite to share it. In fact, spending time in a summer cottage is so highly valued, that rights of use often spark family quarrels!

As the appeal of idling away the hours at their rustic retreats wears off, and memories of Midsummer hangovers begin to fade, Swedes start fishing for more excuses to bring out the **brännvin** (aquavit). And if there's ever a time when the murky bottom of a Swedish lake becomes a source of excitement, it's at the start of the crayfish season. For although the age-old ban on fishing for crayfish between 1st November and the first Wednesday in August was abolished in 1994, the traditional **kräftskiva** celebration associated with the first catch is very popular. These days, however, very few people do their own fishing, and the abundance of cheap, imported crayfish in supermarkets means people can afford to munch their way through mounds of these crustaceans throughout August and well into September.

Things get fishier still with the seasonal premiere for **surström-ming** on the third Thursday in August, but most wrinkle their noses at the thought of consuming this northern Swedish delicacy. Pungent, gassy and tongue-curling, fermented Baltic herring never fails to make an impression. In 2006, several airlines even banned the fish from their carriers, classifying it along with dangerous weapons like shoe bombs and firearms. They argue the cans are pressurised goods and must be classified as potentially explosive. As a result, Arlanda airport has had to stop selling *surströmming*, so you won't be able to take this exotic little treat home with you. And maybe that's for the best!

Inside Out Tip

For all you daredevils out there, a visit to Ullvö Lilla Salteri in the *surströmming* heartland of Örnsköldsvik will be an unforgettable experience. There you can learn all about *surströmming* production and sample the delicacy for yourself. Go to www.surstromming.se for more information.

Seasonal Swedes

INGMAR BERGMAN (14th July 1918 – 30th July 2007) is recognised as one of the greatest and most influential filmmakers of modern cinema, having been Academy Award-nominated nine times. As well as directing 62 films, most of which he also wrote, Bergman directed over 170 plays. Two of his most well-known films are *The Seventh Seal*, which won a Jury Special prize at Cannes in 1957, and *Fanny and Alexander*, which won four Academy Awards in 1983. Well, I never… Bergman's favourite leading ladies were his favourites off-screen too. In addition to his five marriages, Bergman had relationships with Harriet Andersson, Bibi Andersson, and Liv Ullmann, who is also the mother of one of his nine children.

BJÖRN BORG (born in Södertälje on 6th June 1956) rose to tennis stardom in the mid 1970s and is widely regarded as one of the greatest players in the sport's history. Between 1974 and 1981 he won 11 Grand Slam titles, five of which were at Wimbledon and six at the French Open. However, having been defeated by McEnroe at the 1981 US Open, Borg felt he was losing his grip on the No.1 position, and announced his retirement two years later, at the tender age of 26. Although his attempted comeback in the early 1990s failed, Björn Borg's line of clothing and accessories would later recoup some international success. Well, I never… In 2006, Borg put his Wimbledon trophies

Interest in Ingmar Bergman has surged since his death, and the annual Bergman Week taking place on Fårö in the week following Midsummer is increasingly attracting visitors. For more information about Bergman Week and related links, visit www.bergmanveckan.se

and two of his winning rackets up for sale at Bonham's Auction House, prompting a number of players to contact him and express their disbelief. Only when McEnroe called him up to ask if he'd gone mad was he persuaded to buy back the trophies.

STIEG LARSSON (15th August, 1954 – 9th November, 2004) was a Swedish journalist and writer who has achieved international acclaim following the posthumous success of his *Millenium trilogy*. The first of these novels, *The Girl with the Dragon Tatoo* (Swedish title: *Män som hatar kvinnor*) was published in English at the beginnning of 2008. The second, The *Girl who Played with Fire* (Swedish title: *Flickan som lekte med elden*) will be published in 2009 and the third, *Castles in the Sky* (Swedish title: *Luftslottet som sprängdes*) is scheduled for release in 2010. Prior to his sudden death from a massive heart attack, Larsson was chief-editor of the magazine published by the Expo foundation, which monitors anti-democratic, right-wing extremist and racist tendencies in Sweden. Well I never... Stieg Larsson used to spell his first name without an 'e' until he and fellow journalist Stig Larsson flipped a coin to decide who would change his name to prevent confusion in the media. As if having the same name wasn't confusing enough, both were almost the same age, came from the same province in the north of Sweden (Västerbotten) and both would later become reputed authors. Stig Larsson (without the 'e') is a well-known screenwriter, author and film director currently living in Stockholm.

Key words

GYMNASIET Sweden provides a three-year upper-secondary school education after the compulsory nine years of basic schooling, *grundskolan*. Students can study a wide range of vocational or academic subjects within the 17 national programmes on offer, each consisting of eight core subjects plus programme-specific subjects and student electives. These programmes all lead to eligibility for higher education. There are also niche-interest programmes (such as horse management, glassblowing or rescue services) available in just one college, to which anyone from the entire country may apply. Nationwide recruitment also exists for *idrottsgymnasier*, special sports schools where upper-secondary education is combined with training in sports such as football or skiing.

SOMMARSTÄNGT 'Closed for the summer' signs are frequently seen on the doors of small shops and restaurants throughout July.

ALLEMANSRÄTT 'Everyone's right' to move freely through the countryside – an unwritten law dating back to Viking times and still in force throughout Scandinavia. The basic principle is that you can walk, ski, cycle or ride everywhere, so long as nothing is harmed and nobody disturbed.

Although the rules in Sweden, Norway and Finland are not completely identical and there are a variety of restrictions, the following general rights to public access apply:

- You may move through the woods and open landscape and use the lakes and rivers for swimming or boating.
- You may pick wild berries, mushrooms and some kinds of flowers, unless a certain species is protected by law.
- You may camp anywhere for one night (apart from the beach) so long as you do not disturb the local residents.

For more details on Swedish *Allemansrätt* go to www.naturvardsverket.se/en/In-English/Menu and click on Enjoying Nature

BRÄNNVIN A flavoured or unflavoured distilled spirit made from potato or grain, a category which includes aquavit and vodka. Having been brought to Sweden through Hanseatic trade in the 1400s, *brännvin* was originally prized for its medicinal properties.

All the leaves are brown

When the mosquitoes call a cease-fire and the last of the blue-berry pickers emerge from their forest hide-outs, you know autumn has arrived in the Swedish countryside. Quiet wisps of mist swirl through the trees and everything is muted and tranquil. That is, until the hunting season. The sound of quadrupeds shuffling through the undergrowth and the crack of a gun now and again are a sign that things are on the move everywhere.

THE HUNT IS ON

animal	season	regions
Roe deer	Aug–Jan	All
Wild fowl	end Aug–end Jan	All
Moose	Sept–Nov (with a break)	North
Moose	Oct–Nov	South and Central
Beaver	October–mid May	Central and North

The above table is only a general guide as the start and duration of the season for a particular species can vary considerably between one part of the country and another. Foreign hunters should find out through their hosts which dates apply to the area they are visiting. For more information go to: www.jagareforbundet.se/huntinginsweden

In town, things are really stirring too. After a long and indulgent summer break, business is back to normal and it's time to put some of that famous Swedish efficiency into practice. However, as the amount of natural light dwindles, a favourite way to brighten up the day is to gather round candle-lit tables for coffee – **mysigt**!

The saintly glow of 'living light' (as the Swedish for candle light literally translates) is very much in evidence on **allhelgonadagen**. Unlike Halloween, a celebration which has gained in popularity over the past decade and is largely seen as an American import, All Saints' Day has been observed by Swedes for centuries. Even for the irreligious, the Saturday falling between 31st October and 6th November is a time for reflection and paying respects to the dead, and many people visit cemeteries to light candles for deceased relatives.

Did you know that in Sweden, St Martin's Eve is all about eating goose? And since the celebration of Mårtengås on 10th November is largely limited to the province of Skåne, you will have to venture south to sample it.

Inside Out Tip

If you like the idea of being close to nature, but not to the barrel of a gun, a wild life safari at Kolarbyn in Bergslagen will give you all the thrills and none of the spills. Track wolves and moose by moonlight or canoe down river in search of other furry friends, then tell tales of close encounters by a roaring fire back at base camp. Staying in one of the twelve forest huts is a unique experience. For more details go to: www.kolarbyn.se

Wild at heart

From the soft, white beaches of Skåne, up through the dense forests of Värmland and into the craggy hinterland of the North, you'll discover that Sweden really is wild at heart. Since the country's population is small and concentrated in a few towns and cities, vast areas of landscape remain relatively untouched. Sweden also has a long tradition of preserving its natural surroundings, in 1910 becoming the first European country to establish national parks.

Forever green

Although coniferous forest dominates much of the Swedish landscape, deciduous hardwoods such as linden, ash, maple and elm are found throughout Southern Sweden up to the border of Norrland. While other types of vegetation also follow this North-South divide, favourable local climates and soil conditions (such as on the islands of Gotland and Öland and in parts of the Scandinavian mountain range) promote an interesting flora that includes numerous varieties of orchids.

The big five

Undisturbed as they are, the Swedish forests are home to more than moose and roe deer. The wolf, not long ago threatened with eradication, is now expanding its habitat across Northern and Central Sweden, and bear and lynx populations are also increasing.

Due to its remarkable biodiversity, the barren plain of Stora Alvaret on Öland has been designated a UNESCO World Heritage Site.

Guardians of the wilderness

The indigenous people of the Arctic region, the Sámi, have been working hard to revive their culture and identity in recent times. Having suffered a long history of oppression, the people once known as the Lapps began their struggle for increased influence and self-determination in the 1950s. In 1993, the Swedish government granted the formation of *sametinget*, an authoritative body elected by the people, whose task is to safeguard and develop Sámi interests.

Originally nomadic, the Sámi traditionally moved with their reindeer through the seasons, living in tents during the summer and in sturdier peat huts during the winter. Today, they live in more permanent communities and often employ modern methods of herding their animals, such as with helicopters and snow scooters. However, of the 20,000 Sámi living in Sweden, only 10% still make a living from reindeer husbandry, which is often a family business, in many cases combined with tourism or fishing. Urbanization and industrialization of Southern Sweden has contributed to large numbers of the Sámi community moving there in search of more mainstream work opportunities.

Seasonal Swedes

ALFRED NOBEL (21st October 1833 – 10th December 1896) will always be remembered for being pure dynamite. Although the Swedish chemist and engineer used his scientific expertise to further the family armaments business, he was focused on the industrial rather than the military potential of the nitroglycerine-based explosive he patented in 1867. This was duly acknowledged the following year by the Royal Swedish Academy of Sciences, which gave Nobel an honorary award for "important inventions for the practical use of mankind". Having grown old with the kudos of such an achievement but no heirs to his enormous fortune, Nobel was moved to leave the very peaceful legacy of the Nobel Prizes. Well, I never... Nobel was as much of a linguist as he was a scientist, having gained proficiency in the foreign languages of French, Russian, German, Italian and English, in which he was also able to write poetry.

ASTRID LINDGREN (14th November 1907 – 28th January 2002) is undoubtedly the most famous Swedish writer of modern time, her books having been translated into eighty-five languages, to the delight of children and adults alike. The stories about Lindgren's best-loved character, *Pippi Longstocking*, came about as a way of amusing her daughter Karin while she was ill with pneumonia in 1941. However, it was not until a few years later that *Pippi Longstocking* received rave reviews, when the story won

WEATHER WATCH

Early autumn is usually crisp, clear and marvellous – particularly in the north, where the first frosts dramatically intensify the kaleidoscope of turning leaves. This is best seen by road: the often monotonous drive along the E4 from Haparanda to Gävle now becomes a fascinating lesson on how the season gradually sweeps down the country.

Average maximum temperatures

	Sept	Oct	Nov
Stockholm	15	9	5
Gothenburg	16	11	6
Piteå	13	6	0

Fans can visit the Astrid Lindgren World theme park in the author's home town of Vimmerby, Småland.

a children's book competition and launched Lindgren's career. Throughout her lifetime, Astrid Lindgren won many accolades for her work and commitment to social justice, but sadly, the Nobel Prize for Literature eluded her to the end. Well, I never... In 1996, The Russian Academy of Sciences decided to name asteroid 3204 after Astrid Lindgren. Upon hearing the news the author commented: "You'll have to call me Asteroid Lindgren from now on then."

ZLATAN IBRAHIMOVIC (born in Malmö on 3rd October, 1981) has come a long way from rough and ready Rosengård, the largely immigrant neighbourhood of Malmö in which he grew up. The Swedish football striker of Bosnian descent now plays for Italian club, Internazionale, and the Swedish national team. Zlatan has recently achieved a historical first in winning the *Guldbollen* award three times (in 2005, 2007 and 2008). The 'Golden Ball' is awarded by the daily tabloid *Aftonbladet* and the Swedish Football Association to the best male Swedish footballer each year. Well, I never... Zlatan has a reputation for pulling a prank or two. He was once arrested for impersonating a policeman and trying to arrest a kerb-crawler in the red-light district of Malmö, and caused havoc at Stockholm Arlanda airport by asking if a security guard had found his gun.

ANNIKA SÖRENSTAM (born in Stockholm on 9th October 1970) showed sports-star potential from an early age, having excelled at tennis and skiing before switching to golf at the age of 12 and rising through the amateur and professional ranks to become one of the most successful golfers in history. Annika's accumulated earnings from LPGA tournaments amount to over $22 million, putting her at the top of the money list. In 2001, Annika scored 59 in a single round of tournament play - the lowest score in competition by any female player. In 2003, she made history again by being the first woman to play in a men's PGA Tour event since 1945. Well, I never... For the Sörenstams, professional golf is a family affair. Annika and Charlotta Sörenstam are the only two sisters to have both won $1 million on the LPGA.

Key words

MYSIGT If you've ever been obliged to listen to a female Swede's mobile phone conversations on public transport, then you'll have probably heard this word or its grammatical relatives mentioned a few times. Basically meaning 'nice and cosy' it is used to describe a variety of situations which leave you feeling warm and satisfied.

Examples:

Visst var det *mysigt* att gå på bio?
Wasn't going to the cinema nice?   mysigt (adverb)

Men gud, vad *mysigt* det är här!
Oh my, isn't it cosy in here?

Jag håller med, Johan är såå *mysig*
I agree, Johan is just so sweet   mysig (adjective)

Till helgen tänker vi bara *mysa* hemma
We're just going to have a cosy time
at home this weekend   mysa (verb)

Ta på dig dina *mysbyxor* och slappa lite
Put on your slouchy trousers and relax for a bit   mys- (stem component)

The big freeze

To endure a winter as long and dark as Sweden's requires just a little resilience and imagination. Fortunately, cool ideas abound!

The obsession with candles which started in November now reaches a hazardous climax at **Lucia**, on 13th December, when fair maidens' heads are set alight throughout the country. Well, they used to be set alight – Lucia candle crowns tend to be of the battery-driven, plastic kind these days. However, selecting a suitable bearer of the crown is a serious business and no self-respecting town in Sweden will fail to appoint its very own Lucia each year – indeed, many a Miss Sweden started out as a one. Nevertheless, the typical blonde beauty once associated with this privilege is no longer the obvious choice as Swedish society attempts to 'multiculturalise' its traditions.

As one might suspect, the tradition of celebrating Saint Lucia may originally have more to do with keeping the Prince of Darkness at bay than illuminating the world with the Light of Christ. Before the Gregorian calendar was introduced, the date for celebrations coincided with the winter solstice in the Northern hemisphere. Naturally, the longest night of the year was also the scariest, and folklore has it that Lussi, a terrifying female

Inside Out Tip
The run up to Christmas is virtually the only time when Swedes make the effort to have a *smörgåsbord* and then the effort is spent on booking one at a good restaurant. Don't expect your hosts to put on a big spread at home!

demon, would come down the chimney to take away naughty children and lazy people who didn't do their work. So, are the Swedes celebrating a saint who came to the aid of hide-away Christians or are they nodding in the direction of dark forces?

No time to dwell on that little brain-teaser though, because *nu är det **jul** igen** as the famous Swedish Christmas song goes. Yuletide in Sweden incorporates all the usual elements of over-indulgence and family entertainment, but it does have its idiosyncrasies…

Christmas is here again

Did you know that Swedes traditionally put an almond in the pot when making Christmas rice pudding? Superstition has it that the person who is served with the almond will be married the following year.

Tor's goats and little men in red hats

One of the oldest symbols associated with Swedish Christmas is **julbocken** (the Yule Goat), dating back to pre-Christian times when the animal was connected to the Norse god Thor, who rode the sky in a chariot drawn by two goats. *Julbocken's* significance morphed through the ages, until it finally landed the role of gift-bearer in the nineteenth century, when one of the men in the family would dress up as one. The goat was replaced by **jultomten** (Santa Claus) at the end of the century, and the tradition of the man-sized goat disappeared. Since then, *julbocken* has been reduced to a symbolic straw figure, often used as a Christmas tree decoration, but you still sometimes see giant models in town centres – an arsonist's dream.

Jenny Nyström, a Swedish painter and illustrator from the turn of the twentieth century, is widely recognised as having created the classic Swedish *jultomten*. Her figure is friendlier and more gnome-like than that of her German contemporary, Thomas Nast, who is credited with creating the popular image of Santa in the United States. However, the fact that they both clearly draw on Scandinavian folklore is hardly surprising, considering the proximity of their fatherlands.

I'm dreaming of a Swedish Christmas

Lussekatter These feline-shaped saffron buns will have you purring

Lutfisk Curing dried white fish with lye, then soaking and boiling it doesn't sound like a recipe for success, but firm believers in this ancient Christmas treat say the magic is in the sauce

Glögg Yes, we all love this sweet mulled wine, but some of us prefer drier versions with more alcohol

Pepparkakor The perfect accompaniment to glögg, Swedes have fun serving these ginger snaps to foreigners who can't pronounce the word in Swedish

Julskinka Ham today, ham tomorrow and ham the day after. At Christmases past, families tucked into a whole roast pig – at Christmases present they pick away at a supermarket bundle of salt-cured pork – a pallid substitute

Winter is toughest on Southerners, who face a dreary six months of dark, damp and desperately ambivalent cold, as the temperature teeters around zero, but never falls below long enough to allow a comforting blanket of snow to settle. At this time of year, people find these small fluctuations on the Celsius scale fascinating, and will often exclaim things like, '*Oj, det är plusgrader idag!*' (meaning they might consider ditching the woolly hat today) or '*Oj, det är minusgrader idag!*' (meaning they might consider putting on an extra layer of thermal underwear). If such 'plus' and 'minus' reports prior to a walk to the bus stop seem a little silly, their implications for venturing out on the ice of the local lake, however, are not...

Did you know that Swedes excel at designing outdoor gear? Check out www.fjallraven.com and www.houdinisportswear.com or the stockist www.addnature.com

Bird watchers beware! Don't go looking for hot Swedish chicks on their native turf in the middle of winter. They've either migrated for the season to warmer climes or are so swaddled by their Canada goose jackets, you'll barely recognise them.

ICE, ICE BABY...

Långfärdsskridsko – Long distance skating on natural ice – is very popular around the Stockholm archipelago and wherever inland lakes freeze over without having to bear the burden of heavy snow. Gliding along over a vast open space is extremely liberating, and on a sunny day, one of the most enjoyable outdoor activities of the winter. Around the archipelago, you can skate for miles, but read up on your 'ice science' and get the right equipment before embarking on a skating trip. Better still, go with an experienced guide who has a good understanding of ice and weather conditions.

Put your skates on

Vikingarännet – the 'Viking Run' is an annual ice-skating event which was introduced in 1999. In 2003, the ice was fantastic and it was possible for the first time to skate the whole distance (80km) between Uppsala and Stockholm. In other years, poor ice has forced the organisers to cancel or cut short the race. For more information about the event, visit www.vikingarannet.com

Can't get enough of the white stuff? Snow and ice junkies should head to the winter playground of the North! And there's more to it than the world famous Ice hotel in Jukkasjärvi, where tourists bed down under reindeer skins for a sub-zero snooze. From Abisko to Östersund you can have frosty adventures ice-hole fishing, dog sledging and of course, downhill or cross-country skiing.

The Swedish mountains are beautiful, but the skiing they offer cannot be compared with that of their more altitudinous and glamorous Alpine counterparts. However this may be the reason why skiing is a very accessible activity in Sweden – the huge selection of small resorts with no-nonsense facilities are ideal for families.

Your guide to the slippery slopes of Sweden...

Best all round and after ski	Åre	(103 downhill pistes)
Best snow and family skiing	Funäsdalen and environs	(118 downhill pistes)
Best for midsummer skiing	Riksgränsen	(15 downhill pistes)
Best offpiste/heliskiing	Borgafjäll	(13 downhill pistes)

Seasonal Swedes

AUGUST STRINDBERG (22nd January, 1849 – 14th May, 1912) walked on the wild side of literature with his proliferation of plays and stories that shocked Swedish society of the era. A tormented soul at the best of times, Strindberg's addiction to absinthe is said to have heightened his creative intensity – and neuroticism. Despite being far too provocative to collect a Nobel prize in the early 1900s, Strindberg is arguably the most influential and most important of all Swedish authors, and the themes of such masterpieces as *Miss Julie* and the *Dance of Death* keep theatre audiences riveted to their seats to this day. Well I never... Strindberg had a number of eccentric interests – alchemy was one of them. He conducted his experiments at home and once succeeded in making fool's gold, convinced it was the real thing.

Blå tornet (The Blue Tower) on Drottninggatan in Stockholm, was Strindberg's home for the last four years of his life. It is now the Strindberg Museum. For more information visit www.strindbergsmuseet.se

SVEN-GÖRAN ERIKSSON (born in Sunne, on 5th February 1948) has acquired a reputation as The Iceman of the football world, notably for his stint at managing the England team from 2001 – 2006. Replacing the emotionally volatile Kevin Keegan, Eriksson's cool, consensual approach was a breath of fresh air to the players and his steady influence put them back on track for 2002 World Cup qualification. However, it seems 'Eriksson Ice' goes down better in hotter climates: prior to becoming England manager, Eriksson had notable success with the Italian club, Lazio and in 2008, he broke off his contract with Manchester City to become manager of the Mexico national team. Well, I never... Eriksson has better control off pitch than on – the highest level of football he ever played was Division 2 with KB Karlskoga, before being forced to retire prematurely due to a knee injury in 1975.

Having circumnavigated the four seasons, completing our journey in the depths of winter and now thoroughly freezing from top to toe, it's time for a well-deserved pit stop. Knives and forks at the ready...

Down the hatch

In 1992, when I first started living in Umeå as a student, shopping for food was a grim experience. Having come from the supermarket paradise of the UK, I was now confronted with Soviet-like sparsity. Instead of a bread aisle, there was a shelf of rye flour and mysterious-looking syrup; instead of a chilled cabinet full of ready-meals, there was a sad little freezer box containing *Gorbys piroger* (a kind of pasty). Keen to save money, I opted for *fiskbullar* (fish balls) rather than frozen cod, but when I opened the tin of revolting, glutinous gloop, I realised that I would have to can the convenience food and start cooking for real.

Even a Hellenic hero would have paled at my first cookery challenge. As I was casually watching TV in the communal kitchen of my student residence one day, a gruff-looking visitor strode in with a gargantuan sea monster in his arms. 'Can someone do something with this?' he shouted, and dumped ten kilos of evil-looking *Esox lucius* on the kitchen table. Stupidly, I said 'yes'. Half an hour later, I had managed to lacerate both the gigantic pike and my fingers with a blunt Ikea knife, but gave up trying to make a culinary delight of the slimy mess when rubber-dungareed Ronny came back. 'You must take out the guts, you know', he said, grinning, as he unholstered his hunting knife.

WHAT'S LURKING IN YOUR BASKET?

Although supermarkets all over Sweden have improved dramatically over the last fifteen years due to the influences of immigration and travel, grocery shopping can still be a perilous adventure. Look out for:

Messmör Not a type of butter (*smör*) but a soft spread made from whey which is said to be fantastically nutritious. However, the unusual sweetness and texture of *messmör* and its cheesy partner *mesost* is an acquired taste

Kalles kaviar Swedes abroad get homesick for this, but the bright blue tube and rock-bottom price tell you it's a far cry from beluga. The oh-so-salty cod roe favourite is squeezed on to a quarter-of-a-billion open sandwiches each year

Ostkaka Cheese cake by name, not by nature. Don't expect a crumbly biscuit base with this dessert. The traditional Swedish dish is a squidgy mass made by curdling milk with rennet. Delicious warm, with raspberry jam!

Gräddfil/filmjölk OK, you might have worked out what *grädde* and *mjölk* mean, but no-one will thank you for putting the sour versions in their coffee. Swedish sour cream is a popular base for sauces and dips, while the almost infinite varieties of sour milk are eaten for breakfast with fruit jam or muesli

Bruna bönor/ärtsoppa/risgrynsgröt For what can only be purely practical reasons, these three Swedish staples are commonly packaged to look like some obscure kind of sausage. Brown beans (with pork), and pea soup (with pancakes) are traditionally eaten for lunch, but rice pudding is more of a dessert or snack, especially at Christmas

Kroppkakor Old fashioned stodge from the South, 'body cakes' are a challenge to the palate as well as the figure. Anyone for onion and pork dumplings served with butter, cream and jam?

Salta Katten This purrfect little box of black cats is your ideal introduction to the addictive world of ammonium chloride. Better known by its street name *salmiak*, NH_4Cl puts the 'salt' in the salty liquorice which is so popular all over Scandinavia

Limpa Buy one of these loaves and you'll soon discover what the Swedes do with syrup. There are a huge variety of breads going under the name of *limpa* but the one thing they have in common is their sweetness

Mushroom mania. Since 60% of the total land area is forest, and public rights of way rule, Sweden is a mushroom-picker's paradise. Kantareller (chanterelles) are very popular, and widely found throughout the country from July to October, although they are less common in the north. Karl Johan (porcini) are also much prized, as are the more elusive murklor (morels), which grow most abundantly after slash and burn.

No, I did not know, and it took a while before I became more practised at filleting my own fish, shelling prawns, cleaning chanterelles and boiling down blueberries – skills that many Swedes learn from an early age.

Although the idea of cooking **husmanskost** (traditional Swedish food) never really enthused me, eating it did. During my first few frozen winters in the north, there was something very comforting about sitting down to a simple dish of meat or fish, sauce and potatoes. The real joy of it came at midday, however, when I discovered that no-one struggled to eat cheese sandwiches at their desks, but promptly stopped whatever they were doing at 11.55 to join the queue for a hot lunch at the nearest canteen. These rather curious establishments known as **lunchrestauranger** are frequently found close to large businesses and only open during the working week from mid-morning to early afternoon. Once you've recovered from the shock of their furiously efficient, conveyor-belt environments, you'll be pleasantly satisfied with your all-inclusive meal deal.

Did you know there is such a thing as a free lunch? Well in Swedish schools at least, where free meals for all pupils were introduced in 1973.

Let's lunch – surviving the national rush hour

Whether you end up at a canteen or a more expensive restaurant, you'll find having lunch is a serious business in Sweden. And it's rarely a leisurely affair. Sometimes, that precious hour seems to involve more queuing and hanging around for a table than it does eating and relaxing. Still, forewarned is forearmed, so follow the **do's** and **don'ts** below and you'll be well on your way to having a fantastically stress-free lunch:

A weekly **matsedel** (menu) is commonly displayed at restaurant and canteen entrances. Swedes often like to study it in advance to make sure they know exactly what to order each day, thus eliminating the nightmare of in-queue indecision. Some restaurants are so on the ball, they even list their weekly menus on the internet. **Do** decide what you want before joining the queue and have your money ready. **Don't** dawdle – patience at lunch time comes at a premium!

But when is lunch time? Swedes eat early – manual workers often between 10.00-11.30 and everyone else between 11.00-13.00. If you're a stray foreigner looking to lunch after 13.00, expect to be unimpressed by the service – the staff will have started clearing away what's left of the salad bar and won't hesitate to scrape the last few cold potatoes on to your plate. **Do** arrive before 12.00 if you want to be certain of fresh food and a good table. **Don't** bother turning up after 13.30 – you won't be made to feel welcome.

Dagens (dish of the day) is the best value option. For between SEK 60-75, an ordinary Swedish canteen will offer you soup/salad, bread, a hot main course, a cold drink, coffee and biscuits. Most restaurants have similar lunch deals, but coffee might cost extra. **Do** try Swedish dishes for lunch. In the course of a week you could sample five classic meals at a fraction of the price they would cost you in the evening. **Don't** wimp out of the queue to head for the nearest hamburger joint – you'll regret it.

Lingondricka or **lättöl**? Faced with the choice of pink squash or low-alcohol beer, first-timers in a Swedish restaurant might be forgiven for asking for water. However, both lingonberry juice and beer are great drinks to have with husmans. The tart tang of Lingonberry refreshes the palate nicely after a forkful of fried fish, while the beer, low on alcohol but not on taste, takes the cloying richness out of a cream sauce. Years of devising the perfect way to brew this product have served a conscientious society well. **Do** be brave and try *lättöl* – if you have a choice, the brand Spendrups is better than Pripps Blå. **Don't** upgrade to **vin** (wine) or **starköl** (strong beer) when eating with Swedish colleagues. After briefly giving you a blank look of disapproval, they'll jokingly enquire whether you really intend to return to the office later, since breathalysing everyone after lunch is company policy.

Tore Wretman's favourites and other husman must-haves

In Sweden of old, a *husman* was a commoner, living and working on the farm of a richer man. The cheap and basic food he ate came to be known as *husmanskost*, and typically consisted of pork or fish, potatoes and root vegetables. People made do with what they had, without much culinary razzmatazz. At least not until the mid-twentieth century, when the influence of one Swedish restaurateur led to a national revival of traditional Swedish cooking. Suddenly, Swedes were tuning into their radios and switching on their TVs to learn what Tore Wretman had to say about local food and how to cook it. Wretman had advanced from kitchen skivvy at the tender age of sixteen to owner of Riche restaurant at a youthful twenty-nine. By the time he had acquired media fame in the mid 1950s, he was also owner of Operakällaren, which after extensive renovation went on to become one of the most renowned restaurants in Sweden. Wretman's legacy is preserved, not only in the establishments he helped elevate to an internationally high calibre, but also in the consciousness of a new generation of chefs who continue his innovative approach to cooking Sweden's excellent natural produce.

Did you know that there are two authentically Swedish alternatives to the ubiquitous hamburger, pizza and kebab joints? Korvkiosken (the hot dog stand) and the much rarer, strömmingsvagnen (the fried herring 'wagon') are worth a try!

Tore's top three

Kåldolmar Fried parcels of white cabbage containing minced beef and pork mixed with rice

Pannkakor Usually eaten after pea soup, pancakes with strawberry jam are Swedish children's all-time favourite

Skagenröra Wretman's creation is subtly flavoured with dill and lighter than an ordinary prawn mayonnaise – popular as Toast Skagen or with a baked potato

Author's choice

Halstrad strömming Grilled or pan-fried Baltic herring is about as Swedish as it gets. Delicious on *knäckebröd* (crispbread) with potatoes, sour cream, red onion and dill

Pyttipanna Pan-fried cubes of meat and potato with chopped onion (traditionally left-overs) served with a fried egg and pickled beetroot. A creamy version of this dish is called *gräddstuvad pyttipanna*

Lax och potatis The story goes that salmon used to be so cheap and abundant, that Swedish labourers would try to get their employers to agree not to feed them salmon and potatoes more than three times a week. Nowadays, you'd be very lucky indeed to be served Swedish salmon, as most of the fish on the market is farmed in Norway. Nevertheless, modern Swedes love *lax*, whether it's *rökt* (smoked), *gravad* (cured in salt and dill) or simply *kokt* (poached)

And check the menu for

Raggmunk Potato pancake served with bacon and lingonberry – filling and fattening!

Pannbiff The posh cousin of the famous *köttbullar* (Swedish meatballs), pannbiff is essentially a pan-fried beef patty served with potatoes and an onion sauce

Dillkött Eating this old-fashioned dish of boiled veal or lamb with a cream and dill sauce will transport you back to yesteryear

Fans of the cheese sandwich need not despair, as the average working day in Sweden is punctuated by **fika**, a coffee break in which chocolate-chip cookies tend to be rejected in favour of the **smörgås** (sandwich), simply consisting of one slice of bread with a savoury topping. However, *fika* doesn't give you licence to rush off and do some last-minute photocopying before your PowerPoint presentation. It should be spent socialising and liaising with colleagues – which is why a whole fifteen to twenty minutes is devoted to the exercise, usually twice a day!

The Swedes' love of *fika* spills out of the office and into the streets, where café culture flourishes, albeit in a restrained 9-5 fashion. Traditional **konditori** (bakeries) are great for experiencing older café customs, such as drinking **bryggkaffe** (Swedish filter coffee) instead of a cappuccino, or eating **kanelbullar** (cinnamon buns) rather than blueberry muffins. Unfortunately, the Swedish saying, *smakar det så kostar det* ('If you like it, it'll cost you') is very true of going out for *fika*, when you can often spend more on coffee and cake than you do on lunch.

Did you know *Fika is the name of a Swedish espresso bar on 58th Street in New York? Neil Armstrong, Monica Lewinsky, and Renée Zellweger count among the café's clientèle, while Håkan Mårtensson, Swedish gold medallist at the 2008 Culinary Olympics has recently been recruited to enhance the variety of delectables on offer.*

Inside Out Tip

Kanelbulle virgins should head to Café Saturnus for their first bite of a Swedish cinnamon bun. The stylish hangout on Eriksbergsgatan in Stockholm boasts the biggest, softest *kanelbullar* you could ever desire.

Konditori classics

Smörgåstårta   A rich sandwich 'cake' made up of several layers of bread with creamy fillings such as egg and mayonnaise, liver pâté, prawns, ham, fish roe and smoked salmon. One piece of this is guaranteed to stave off hunger for hours!

Punschrullar   Affectionately nicknamed *dammsugare* because they are shaped like old-fashioned cylinder vacuum cleaners and filled with the crumbs left over from making other cakes, these arrack-flavoured marzipan rolls are terrific little treats to have with coffee

Prinsesstårta   Created in the 1930s by famous cookery teacher, Jenny Åkerström, this vanilla and whipped cream sponge, encased in green marzipan was a particular favourite of princesses Margaretha, Märtha and Astrid – hence the name 'Princess Cake'. It continues to be the people's favourite on occasions such as birthdays and office parties

Indulgence on a shoestring

With most people feeling flush on pay day, the end of the month is a busy time for pubs and restaurants. But because swanky nights out also leave them feeling out of pocket, those ever-practical Swedes often fall back on more traditional and cheaper ways of living it up.

Plankstek Snobby Stockholmers might turn up their noses at such a provincial favourite, but made with good **oxfilé** (beef fillet) this steak and duchess potato extravaganza served on a wooden board will certainly put you in the party mood. Commonly advertised as a meal deal with a glass of wine or strong beer at the local **krog** (pub) – for example, **plankstek + ett glas rött/stor stark 95:-**

Finlandsfärjan A Baltic sea crossing on the 'Finland ferry' is the mini-break of choice for east coast Swedes eager to let their hair down on a tax-free budget. Infamously supportive of 'vodka belt' drinking habits, these crossings appeal to people of all ages, whether they're sweet young things hankering after a night of cheap cocktails and Eurodisco, or pensioners who take the breakfast buffet seriously and are intent on downing as many Irish coffees as they can before disembarkation.

Inside Out Gourmet Tip

There are plenty of stately homes open to the public in Sweden, but few as atmospheric and welcoming as Yxtaholm in Södermanland. Its proximity to Stockholm has made it a favoured venue for diplomatic negotiations, while full hotel and conference facilities attract business and leisure visitors alike. As well as boasting a wonderful restaurant which offers exquisitely prepared local produce, Yxtaholm has the largest collection of calvados outside of France. It is also home to a unique Arabian horse stud farm, from which hotel guests can arrange to ride out into the stunning Södermanland countryside. For more information go to www.yxtaholm.se

By all means rush off and buy a ticket for this experience of a life time, but please bear in mind you'll be spending more than twelve hours with people in various states of pre- and post-inebriation. Baltic Bliss or Baltic Blues? You decide… For booking information go to www.vikingline.se

Vargtass   'Wolf's paw' is a mean drink, especially if it's made the traditional northern way – with moonshine and that beloved left-over from lunch, *lingondricka*. These days, however (perhaps thanks to the Finland ferry) it's more likely to be based on **Absolut Vodka** than a dodgy home-made brew. Nevertheless, while *vargtass* remains a symbol of homespun boozing, Absolut vodka has become a highly sophisticated international brand seen in all the best cocktail bars

Snus   For a smoke-free nicotine fix Swedes love *snus* (oral tobacco). First-time users beware, however – the instant and very potent hit is enough to knock even the toughest Gauloise-smoker sideways

By the end of the week, though, no-one seems too worried about letting a few hundred-kronor notes fly, if not in a coffee shop, then at **Systembolaget**, where Friday afternoon queues for the weekend's supply of alcoholic beverages are notorious. Sweden's alcohol monopoly has endured and is indeed thriving, despite the more relaxed EU import regulations of recent years. It seems the novelty of driving down to Denmark to stock up on cheap beer and spirits is wearing off, even in the southern counties of Skåne, Blekinge and Halland. And foreigners who initially find it annoying when they can't pick up a bottle of Chardonnay at the supermarket, soon realise the range of wines and expertise on offer at *Systembolaget* somehow makes up for this purchasing restriction. Sometimes.

Suitably re-fuelled, our thoughts might be turning to the delights and cultural diversions of the city. Let's investigate…

Inside Out Tip

Avoid *matlagningsvin* at all costs! This alcohol-free, 'cooking wine' is found in Swedish supermarkets, where beverages containing more than 3.5% alcohol by volume legally cannot be sold. Although the label claims otherwise, *matlagningsvin* is a gruesome substitute for real wine and will kill your cuisine!

Systembolaget is one place where youthful looks are a hindrance not a help. If staff are in any doubt that you might be under the legal purchasing age of 20, they will ask you for ID.

A tale of three cities

Board any train from Stockholm and within thirty minutes of your departure you'll be struck by how quickly the urban landscape ebbs away into a blur of pine trees and wind-swept plains. Travel west towards Gothenburg to find the scenery occasionally interrupted by clusters of red houses, after which the train might stop at a small station platform, perhaps with some evidence of a town centre behind it. Journey south towards Malmö and the story is similar.

Indeed, population density outside the capital drops so sharply, that describing communities in the rest of the country as towns and cities becomes something of an exaggeration. Officially, the term *stad* refers to any locality in Sweden with a population in excess of 10,000. While the list of such towns/cities is long, only twelve have more than 100,000 inhabitants* and just three merit status as storstad (metropolis). Moreover, current population growth is almost solely confined to these three regional hubs. Let's ponder a little on what makes them such people-magnets...

*Statistics Sweden, December 2007

Malmö – gateway to the continent

Having rested on its solid shipping industry past, Malmö was hard hit by the recession of the mid 1970s, the closure of Kockum shipyard a decade later marking the end of an era. Today, Malmö is a flagship of Swedish regeneration, its docklands home to bold new residential developments, IT industries and Malmö University.

PULL FACTORS

International atmosphere In the city quarter of *Möllevången*, where some streets have the colourful, multi-cultural feel of London's Edgware Road.

Music vibe Definitely the rougher and edgier of the three cities, Malmö is famous for its rock scene. Kulturbolaget (KB) on Friisgatan has been a crowd-pulling venue for over twenty years.

Öresundsbron The concept of trans-national regional development has materialised with the building of the Öresund Bridge. Danes are buying cheaper houses in Skåne* and Swedes are seeking better work opportunities in Sjælland.** With Copenhagen now only thirty-five minutes away by train, Malmö really is the gateway to the continent. *A.k.a Scania ** A.k.a Zealand

Did you know Kockums is now a naval stealth specialist, manufacturing submarines and other vessels as part of ThyssenKrupp marine systems? Kockums actually built its first submersibles in 1914.

FAST FACTS

• Malmö city proper is a small *storstad*, with a population of just over 280,000. However, the new Öresund region comprising Skåne (in Sweden), and Sjælland, Lolland-Falster and Bornholm (in Denmark), is home to 3.6 million people, 70% of whom live in the Greater Malmö-Copenhagen area, making it the largest conurbation in Scandinavia.

• Skåne belonged to the Danes until 1658 and disputes over its true nationality have raged ever since, most recently (but perhaps less seriously) in 2007 when an *Aftonbladet* newspaper poll revealed that 51% of participants thought Sweden should give the province back to Denmark.

Turning Torso, Santiago Calatrava's creation in the Western Harbour of Malmö is the tallest building in Scandinavia and the second-highest residential structure in Europe (after Triumph-Palace, Moscow).

Thank you for the music...

Pop music has always been one of Sweden's strongest exports, whether we associate it with the past success of **Abba** and **Roxette** or the current buzz around **Robyn** and up-and-coming **Lykke Li**. Nevertheless, Swedes have had international smash hits in different genres over the years – remember these?

Madonna move over – here comes Robyn

The Final Countdown (1986) The rock band **Europe** started out life in Upplands Väsby (outside Stockholm) in the early eighties, but by the end of the decade, had toured the world. After a twelve-year break, the band reassembled in 2003 and are rocking the globe once more.

Buffalo Stance (1989) **Neneh Cherry** rapped her way to the top of the American dance chart with this club hit, classy collaborations with the likes of **Massive Attack** and **Youssou N'Dour** later preserving her street cred. Musical talent runs in the family – half-siblings **Eagle Eye** and **Titiyo** are both successful singers.

Big Big World (1998) **Emilia's** hit single sold over 4 million copies and then we all wondered what happened to her world. Having gathered new momentum in 2007 with a fresh album, Miss Rydberg set her sights on Eurovision fame, and finished ninth in the 2009 national competition.

With the word *Eurovision* thus indelibly inked on the page, it would be inexcusable not to mention Sweden's love affair with this song contest, which is nationally embraced as **melodifestivalen**. Winning hits through the decades such as *Waterloo*, *Diggy-loo diggy-ley*, *Fångad av en stormvind* (*Captured by a Love Storm*) and *Take Me to Your Heaven* have fuelled a peculiarly Swedish fascination with **schlager** – catchy pop music of the Eurovision kind. If you're in any doubt about what that means, a Saturday-night visit to *Lemon Bar* on Scheelegatan in Stockholm will clarify things.

But on another note, or shall we say foot, you could always go in search of **dansbandsmusik**, especially if you're a fan of foxtrot and lindy hop. Swedish 'dance band' music has roots in country, pop, rock and swing, its style influenced by whatever is most popular at the time. In this regard, there are also regional preferences: from the slow, country numbers of the South, stepping up to snappier *bugg** tunes in the middle of Sweden and faster rock rhythms in the North. To sample some, go to www.dansbandsdax.se and click on *lyssna* (listen).
*Swedish style bugg is a little different to jitter bug/lindy hop

Needless to say, there's more to the Swedish music scene than *schlager* and *dansband*. Here are some names you may or may not recognise:

E.S.T (jazz) **Ann Sofie von Otte**r (opera) **Sofia Jannok** (Sámi ballads) **Hird** (club/electro) **Kaah** (soul/r'n'b) **The Hives** (garage-punk)

Did you know *there's an entire museum dedicated to Abba? Although a permanent site for the unique exhibition has yet to be found, dancing queens everywhere will be thrilled to learn that Abba the Museum is set for a world tour beginning in 2009. For more details see www.abbamuseum.com*

Gothenburg's got it!

Years of being Stockholm's little brother hasn't crushed Gothenburg's self-esteem, despite condescending attitudes occasionally emanating from the capital. In fact, all that east coast jibing is probably rooted in envy. Here's why:

PULL FACTORS

Cheerful bustle For day-trippers, Gothenburg is charming and accessible, its cohesive urban centre much more easily negotiated than Stockholm's 'city of islands'. Added bonuses are the trams* and *Älvsnabben*, a speedy ferry service which regularly traverses the river, Göta Älv. On the street, Gothenburg exudes a cheeriness that Stockholm lacks, whether it's part of the friendlier service in bars and restaurants, or the more satisfying shopping experience, even true of the gigantic mall, *Nordstan*.

Stockholm is itching to reinstate its tram service, which fell out of use in 1967.

Gastronomy/night life Gothenburg's rising reputation as the epicurean epicentre of Scandinavia is well-deserved. From mid-priced brasseries to Michelin star-rated restaurants, the city's gastro-buzz is unmistakable, not least because local culinary talents are achieving international fame. Follow up your meal in style at the innovatively designed *Göteborgsoperan*, or at *Glow*, just one of the many clubs along *Avenyn*.

FAST FACTS
- Gothenburg is the second largest city in Sweden, with a population of approximately 500,000, and a further 400,000 in its metropolitan environs. The Göteborg Region as a whole is strong on technology-based industries, supported by Gothenburg's logistic advantages as the largest port in Scandinavia.

- The southern Gothenburg archipelago is mentioned in the Norse sagas as *Elfarsker* (the river islets) due to its location at the mouth of the Göta Älv. Centuries after vikings paddled these waters, the craggy seascape now tempts tourists to enjoy their own maritime adventures, albeit on lobster safari rather than in longboat warfare.

Big is beautiful Perhaps Gothenburg's engineering instincts have helped the city think big, making it home to:

Liseberg – the largest amusement park in Scandinavia

The Gothia Cup – the world's largest youth soccer competition. In 2008, 1,570 teams from 61 countries participated

Sahlgrenska University Hospital – the largest hospital in Northern Europe with around 2,700 beds and 17,000 employees

---

Did you know that the Gothenburg group Ace of Base is in the Guinness Book of Records? Their album Happy Nation is the world's best-selling debut album, having sold twenty-three million copies.

Design rules

Swedish design has recently seen a shift away from the spartan functionality that has long been its hallmark. A desire to tell a story and rediscover the figurative is at the heart of this rebellion – a rebellion that might also reflect changing attitudes towards a creative ethos anchored in the ideals of the twentieth-century welfare state. This change can be detected in all areas of design from furniture to fashion, in the floral extravagance of a new *IKEA* armchair or the puff sleeves on a *Fillipa K* jacket. Nevertheless, the Swedish love of clean lines remains, and the result of marrying new boldness with traditional values has lead to some exciting developments. Take a look at…

Orrefors and Kosta Boda glassware

The two most famous names in **Glasriket** (Kingdom of Crystal) have been part of the same group since 1990. The *Orrefors limited collection* is a showcase of beautiful experimentation, while *Bertil Vallien* at *Kosta Boda* consistently impresses. Go to www. glasriket.se to find out more about Småland's sparkling treasures.

CKR architecture and design

The design trio started out in architecture but are now multidisciplinary, their achievements including the *Sfera Building* in Kyoto, set design for Kylie Minogue and the *Eve bracelet*, which won a *Design S* award in 2008. Visit www.claesson-koivisto-rune. se to view their full portfolio.

Bertil Vallien carafe

Odd Molly tunic

Odd Molly fashion

Brought together for collaboration on an advertising project in 2002, freelance designer Karin Jimfelt-Ghatan and word artist Per Holknekt ended up conspiring creatively on a completely different tack – their range of pretty, bohemian clothes which are an "accidentally perfect mismatch." The label is a big international success already. More info at www.oddmolly.com

And to get an overview of the latest in Swedish design...

Check out www.swedishdesignaward.se The new Design S award is intended to reflect the best Swedish design in a wide range of fields.

Browse the colourful Designtorget stores for gifts that are novel, innovative and functional. Designtorget's slogan "New, hand-picked items. Every week." inspires confidence in the variety of goods for sale, as does its policy of adjusting stock according to customer-demand. Find stores in major cities around the country or buy online at www.designtorget.se

Visit the Formex design exhibition Nordic design pilgrims regularly attend this event in Stockholm. For more information go to www.formex.se

Stockholm – under construction

It might not be as hip as Copenhagen, or as kooky as Oslo, but Stockholm has the bureaucratic balls to brand itself 'Capital of Scandinavia'. And in a sudden rush to make itself worthy of that title, it has turned into a construction site – complete with major road diversions, acres of scaffolding and newspaper hype about skyscraper ambitions. For a city of just over 800,000 inhabitants, its Vision 2030* is going to be a tough one to realise, and perhaps symptomatic of a 'head on a stick' tendency to focus on the needs of the capital at the expense of the rest of the country.

*for more details see www.stockholm.se

But cynicisms aside, Stockholm is already pretty fabulous, as the growing number of visitors, students and new inhabitants will tell you.

PULL FACTORS

Quality of life Water, water everywhere must be Stockholm's number-one selling point. The fact that you can kayak your way through the city or stroll around its islands along picturesque, waterside paths, gives its residents a sense of liberation denied many urbanites elsewhere. Add to that a clean environment and a good public transport system and you can begin to see why Stockholm ranked among the top ten most liveable cities in *Monocle Magazine*'s Global Quality of Life Survey, 2008.

FAST FACTS
- Although Stockholm has a small population as far as capital cities go, the county as a whole sprawls some distance and is home to almost two million people. The Stockholm region (comprising the four administrative counties of Stockholm, Sörmland, Västmanland and Uppsala) accounts for approximately 35% of Sweden's GDP.

- Prior to Stockholm's rise as the capital of Sweden in the thirteenth century, the settlements around Lake Mälaren were important from an economic and political perspective, notably Birka and later Sigtuna, the latter being the seat of Sweden's first royal mint. Birka is a UNESCO world heritage site, its fascinating archaeological findings from the Viking Age attracting visitors from around the globe.

Economic growth This is where the jobs are. According to the European Regional Innovation Scoreboard 2006, the Stockholm region, followed by that of Gothenburg, are leading European centres of innovation.

Arts scene incubator *Dramatiska Institutet* (film, radio, television and theatre studies) and *Konstfack* (arts, crafts and design) are just two of Stockholm's university colleges that are attracting international students to their degree programmes taught in English. Both colleges have ultra-modern campuses, providing their students with the best multi-disciplinary environments in which to be creative. And for culture vultures in general, let's not forget *Kulturhuset*, the massive arts centre in the middle of Stockholm, which has been working hard since 1974 to provide a forum for photography, design and the performing arts. Its youth and children's initiatives are particularly popular.

Did you know that there is only one 24-hour pharmacy in Stockholm? Apoteket Scheele on Klarabergsgatan (near the central station). Privatisation of the pharmacy sector at the beginning of 2009 may change things...

The tourist triangle: explore the nooks and crannies of Gamla Stan (roof tops) before taking a guided tour of the Royal Palace (left) then finish your day at Nationalmuseum (across the water).

Inside Out capital special

Over a million tourists visit Stockholm each year, attracted by its beauty and cultural points of interest. Stockholm Visitors Board has done a great job of compiling information about the capital, their website www.stockholmtown.com telling you everything you need to know about its museums, theatres, exploring the archipelago and more. But once you've trodden the cobbled streets of Gamla Stan or circuited Stureplan a few times, you may find yourself in need of a little Inside Out inspiration.

What to do when...

IT'S A DARK AND MISERABLE, RAINY AFTERNOON

Start off in erudite fashion by going to *Kulturhuset* to browse their comics and graphic literature library *Serieteket*, before taking a window seat in the fifth floor Café Panorama to sip coffee and gaze down at the goings on at *Sergels torg*. Next, brave the rain again for a short walk down to Strömkajen where you can suitably reward yourself with a stylish cocktail in *The Cadier Bar* at the *Grand Hôtel*. You might have just stepped in out of the cold, but the bar staffs' impeccable service will make you feel warm and welcome. By the time you've downed your drink, the cinemas will have opened, and what better way to spend the hours before dinner than at one of Stockholm's more artsy film theatres? Choose *Zita* (Birger Jarlsgatan) for independent and international cinema or *Skandia* (Drottninggatan) for its historically marvellous interior. Note, this is all best experienced on a weekday – avoid *Kulturhuset* at the weekends, if you can.

YOU FIND YOURSELF IN SHOPPING MALL HELL

Stockholmers don't seem to care that their indoor shopping centres are boring, they just keep on building them – bigger, brasher and with exactly the same shops as before. Perhaps it's something to do with the weather and a love of practical solutions – if you can buy everything you need under one roof, why bother with the High Street? However, for those of you trying to muffle screams as you're dragged along to *Gallerian*, its evil underlings *Sturegallerian* and *Västermalmsgallerian* or even worse, the out-of-town super star, *Kista galleria*, relax – there are alternatives:

Åhléns City and NK (city centre)
Traditional department stores which know what they're doing and improving all the time

Götgatan (Södermalm)
This street and its off-shoots just get better – variety is the spice of life

Hantverkargatan (Kungsholmen) and Rörstrandsgatan (Vasastan)
Perhaps not the most hip and happening of shopping streets, but the small boutiques in these pockets of the city where time has stood still will give you a flavour of Stockholm half a century ago in a way other areas don't. Hantverkargatan is good for vintage clothing and bric-a-brac, Rörstrandsgatan for the cafés

YOU SPONTANEOUSLY DECIDE TO GO OUT ON THE TOWN
A tricky one, as Stockholm night life rarely rewards spontaneity – you're in the Capital of Planning, remember? Nevertheless, it is possible to zig-zag across the city on a whim and party into the early hours, without wads of cash and a sexy entourage, as long as you avoid the obvious Stureplan traps (Spybar, for example). A few places to try on the spur of the moment, of a less-serious-club, more-stylish-hangout nature:

Och Himlen Därtill, Skrapan, Götgatan 78
Good time to go: Early, for pre-dinner cocktails
Atmosphere: Mixed crowd, stylish but easy-going
It's somewhat ironic that a building which was once the dead centre of dullness (as HQ for the Swedish tax office) has become such a landmark of liveliness. Renovated in 2007 to accommodate students and a 'different' kind of shopping centre, the top two floors of the twenty-six storey building were turned into a panoramic bar and restaurant. The drinks are pricey but then you are paying a premium for the spectacular 360° view of Stockholm

Hotellet, Linnégatan 18
Good time to go: Any time before midnight
Atmosphere: Urban chic, Generation X
Thus named because it was originally going to be a hotel, Hotellet is surprisingly less pretentious and more welcoming than most of its Stureplan counterparts. And the welcome continues inside, where the chic layout on two levels makes migrating from cocktail bar to dance floor a very congenial experience. Great for after-work drinks and dinner, but you could quite easily stay on for the house music later

Spy on the streets of Söder-malm from Skrapan.

Allmänna Galleriet 925, Kronobergsgatan 37
Good time to go: After dinner, for drinks before 23.00
Atmosphere: Arty but friendly, mixed crowd
Part of the charm of going to 'AG' is finding the place – very surreptitiously located two floors up from an unmarked street entrance next to a blue movie store. But once inside, the mix of old-fashioned leather sofas and the surprise of whatever temporary art installation is there at the time will not disappoint. The restaurant is excellent

Petsounds Bar, Skånegatan 80
Good time to go: Any time before 23.00
Atmosphere: Relaxed Indie rock
Petsounds record shop is famous for its wide selection of music, on vinyl as wells as CD. Once you've finished browsing the store you can pop across the street to have a meal in the bar before going down to the basement to drink beers and immerse yourself in the latest Swedish sounds. The DJs on both floors really know their stuff

So you've tasted the food, seen the sights and met the locals. Perhaps it's time to be a little more adventurous and get to grips with the lingo...

Can you Swinglish?

A London stockbroker once hired me to teach him Swedish so that he could understand the chit-chat outside of the board-room when he was dealing in Stockholm. Apparently, his Scandinavian colleagues had decided that English was for official business only, and their informal, native language 'friendlies' were unimportant to him. The stockbroker thought otherwise and I agreed.

Similar scenarios are familiar around the globe, as non-native speakers become more adept at switching the 'on' and 'off' button for English to suit the situation and a new generation becomes more confident in using English as a lingua franca. In the Scandinavian countries, such confidence is merited, as the overall standard of English as a second language is high. But in Sweden at least, this can lead to a rather dismissive approach to visitors doing their best to try a few words of Swedish, sometimes because Swedes fail to realise that you actually want to learn their language and sometimes because they are a bit too eager to practice their English.

Nevertheless, the next time a Swede insists on speaking to you in *engelska* despite your Berlitz phrase book attempts to converse in *svenska*, take comfort: Swedes do slip up, a lot of their more amusing mistakes having to do with 'false friends', words that could be confused in English and Swedish because they look like they mean the same thing. At other times, literal translation is the hardened hooligan behind some of the biggest linguistic crimes.

It should come as no surprise then if…

YOU HEAR THINGS LIKE THIS	AND FIND YOURSELF THINKING
My house is two miles away from here.	A brisk two-mile walk or a twenty-kilometre trek? If it's *Swedish miles* away, I'd try to arrange transport.
It's very funny to skate on the lake.	That might be true if you're Bambi on ice. Although it could be a whole lot of *fun* too.
The VD will be with you shortly.	I hope not – but do ask the *MD* to hurry up.
He's my chief.	So which tribe are you then, Sioux or Navajo? These days *bosses* are the same all over the world, don't you think?
I'll follow you.	I appreciate security is a concern, but please go *with* me instead.
I like wandering about in the nature.	Really? I find a nice stroll *in the countryside* does it for me.
I want a bloody steak	Now, how *rare* is that? I think I'll have the f***ing fish!

What's in a name?

Bored with *Svensson*, *Eriksson*, *Karlsson* or any other Scandinavian surname suffixed *-son*, Swedes are increasingly deciding to change their names to something more exciting, particularly when they get married (yes, marriage is becoming more popular too). However, choosing a suitable name in Sweden can be a tricky business, as Jan Gustavsson and Åsa Kristoffersson* found out when they decided to adopt a single family name on the birth of their first child. Unable to take the ancestoral name *Larm* because it wasn't on the church records, or *Ugglum* because the Swedish Names Act doesn't allow the use of a place name for a person, the couple finally settled on *Sturestig* – Sture and Stig the first names of Åsa's and Jan's fathers respectively. Sounds like a trend-setting twist on the viking tradition.

Originally reported on in the local newspaper, Mitt I Kungsholmen

Some examples of first names disallowed by the Swedish Patent and Registration Office:

Asterix (a title of someone else's copyright literary or artistic work)

Lovejoy (someone else's business name or trademark that is copyright in Sweden)

Donadoni (a generally known foreign surname)

Montana (a name that may be understood as a place name)

Top ten most popular names for girls and boys born in 2008 (Statistics Sweden):

1.	Maja	Lucas
2.	Emma	Oscar
3.	Julia	William
4.	Ella	Elias
5.	Elsa	Hugo
6.	Alice	Alexander
7.	Alva	Erik
8.	Linnea	Isak
9.	Wilma	Filip
10.	Klara	Emil

Having abandoned the phrase book and found your bearings in the land where the question, 'Do you speak English?' is almost redundant, your next challenge is to spot the Anglicisms in the Swedish. There are so many of these already, that you could find yourself inventing new ones and getting away with it!

Some English loan words and Anglicised verbs with their more 'correct' Swedish alternatives

maila (to email)	e-posta, mejla
press release	pressmeddelande
printa ut (print out)	skriva ut
airbag	krockkudde
design	formgivning
shoppa* (go shopping)	handla

*Here, context dictates whether or not to use the Anglicised verb, for example:

Jag vill shoppa lite kläder	I want to go clothes shopping
Jag vill handla lite mat	I want to do some food shopping

So *shoppa* is used when shopping is perceived to be a leisure activity, not a chore!

And that's part of the fun, because you'll find the Swedes an accommodating bunch, whether you can *Swinglish* or not.

Sweden is a country of people willing to absorb new influences, linguistic and otherwise. They are curious to learn new things, improve and make a difference to the outside world – even though that outside world sometimes gets confused about who they are. Moreover, they want to share with you the best of what they have: those pristine lakes and pine forests but also a new spirit of freedom and integration.

It is this new spirit that somehow makes the answers to our original questions hazy – are the Swedes really 'conflict-shy', 'reserved', and 'unemotional', or are multi-cultural influences slowly reshaping the nation and our subsequent view of what is characteristically Swedish? The past is not the present, and the present is not the future.

So now that your snapshot briefing is over, visit, revisit and judge Sweden for yourself. From Inside Out, it's over and out.

Inside Out Tip

If you're interested in learning Swedish in Sweden, a course at *Folkuniversitetet*, an adult educational association may be your best option. There are branches all over the country with a wide range of professionally-oriented and qualification-driven courses. Go to www.folkuniversitetet.se for more details.

Photographs
NordicPhotos except
p 17, 41 Scanpix
p 27 Boklok
p 63 Lars Gabrielsson
p 65 Skogens konung
p 71 Astrid Lindgrens värld
p 83 Jonas Kullman
p 95 Tine Guth Linse
p 101 AnnaKarin Drugge
p 105 HSB Turning Torso, Pierre Mens
p 106 Kosta Boda
p 107 Odd Molly
p 119 Skrapan

Bibliography
In addition to sources mentioned in the text, the following
works and websites were consulted:

Sweden, the nation's history, Franklin D.Scott (University
of Minnesota Press, 1977), http://www.bbc.co.uk/history,
http://www.sweden.se, http://www.dn.se, http://www.svd.se
http://www.wikipedia.org

*A thousand thanks (as they say in Sweden) to my editor,
Sharon for her timely advice, and to Johnny for all his terrific suggestions.*